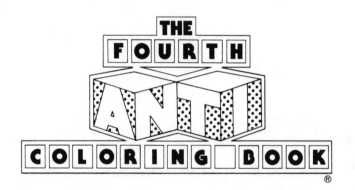

THE FOURTH ANTI COLORING BOOK

THE FOURTH ANTI COLORING BOOK

Susan Striker

®

HOLT, RINEHART and WINSTON   New York

To Herberta W. Sinkus

"Your chance is not my chance."
–Marcel Duchamp

Published by Holt, Rinehart and Winston, 383 Madison Avenue,
New York, New York 10017.
Published simultaneously in Canada by Holt, Rinehart and Winston
of Canada, Limited.
ISBN: 0-03-057872-8
First Edition

Printed in the United States of America
10   9   8   7   6   5   4   3   2   1

Illustrations by Joe Dyas, Judy Francis, Steve Hall, James Janey,
Randi Katzman, Maggie MacGowan, Susan Striker, and David Vozar.

The Anti–Coloring Book is a registered trademark of Susan Striker.

Introduction

I recently bought a present for the three-year-old son of a police officer. I thought I had found the perfect gift—a bright red police car "just like Daddy's." Wrappings were excitedly removed and batteries inserted, and when the car took off across the living room, was I ever embarrassed. The car did all the playing and left poor Tony sitting there with nothing to do. It backed up, unaided, whenever it encountered a wall or chair leg. The siren wailed and lights flashed authentically, with no help from the child. I might just as well have given Tony a coloring book as that car, since both equally discourage exploratory play and creative expression.

Like coloring books, more and more toys currently manufactured stifle a child's self-expression. It is little wonder our children seem to be getting fatter and duller as their toys get cleverer and do more for them. Toys play by themselves; television replaces daydreaming and reading; hand-held electronic "action" games simulate a good work-out for sitting football "players." Instead of doing the imagining, thinking, and problem-solving involved in drawing, children find they need only connect dots, or color in an adult-drawn picture, or paint by number, or cover an already painted picture with plain water to "magically" see the painting.

In previous *Anti–Coloring Books* I have written about how detrimental coloring books are to a child's creative expression. Teachers, parents, and psychologists generally agree on this point, and yet there are still some early childhood teachers who justify giving their students color-in worksheets with the misconception that "it improves fine motor skills" needed for penmanship. Actually, coloring-in works against this development. As Dr. Robert J. Saunders, art teacher and consultant to the Connecticut State Department of Education, has said, "Drawing leads to good penmanship; the coloring-in of predrawn shapes and outlines does not."

Providing children with opportunities for creative expression is crucial to their development. It helps to shape their self-image, teaches them to think independently, and forms their approach to problem solving. I strongly hope that the *Anti–Coloring Books* not only provide children with some pleasurable activities, but also help foster the kind of stimulus that seems to be getting rarer in our children's world. It is important for parents who endorse the philosophy that rejects coloring books to reexamine toys they buy for their children in the same light, and to pass up the clever toy in favor of the simple toy that encourages the child to be clever.

What do you need a fairy godmother to do for you?

**What would it look like if
you could see what a skunk smelled like?**

News

30¢

November 3

Vol. CXXX

NEW SUPERHERO!

Superman, Wonder Woman, and Spiderman meet to congratulate new Superhero.

cynthio olnunlchy nlchy oho llol yllo lucynollo du cynthio ol lnun clu don clhonl clhonh luc yln un r cluo ynllonlc lnun clu du /lonulio oh oulh noulh nlnonyic oun lonlo nlh r cllo yllonulio o u olo yllnol lyu or lyu on lnucn yun lnoqu llnoc ouy olo yllnc

World astonished by impressive feats of Superhero.

/lonulio oh ou lr noulh nlnonyic oun lonlo nlh r cllo yllonulio o r olo yllnol lyu or lyu on lnucn yun lnoqu llnoc ouy olo yllnc cynthio olnunlchy nlchy oho llol yllo lucynollo du cynthio ol lnun clu don clhonl clhonh luc yln un r cluo ynllonlc lnun clu du llonulio oh oulh noulh nlnonyic oun lonlo nlh r cllo yllonulio o

© Susan Striker

You are a famous pilot flying on an important mission.

What's the catch?

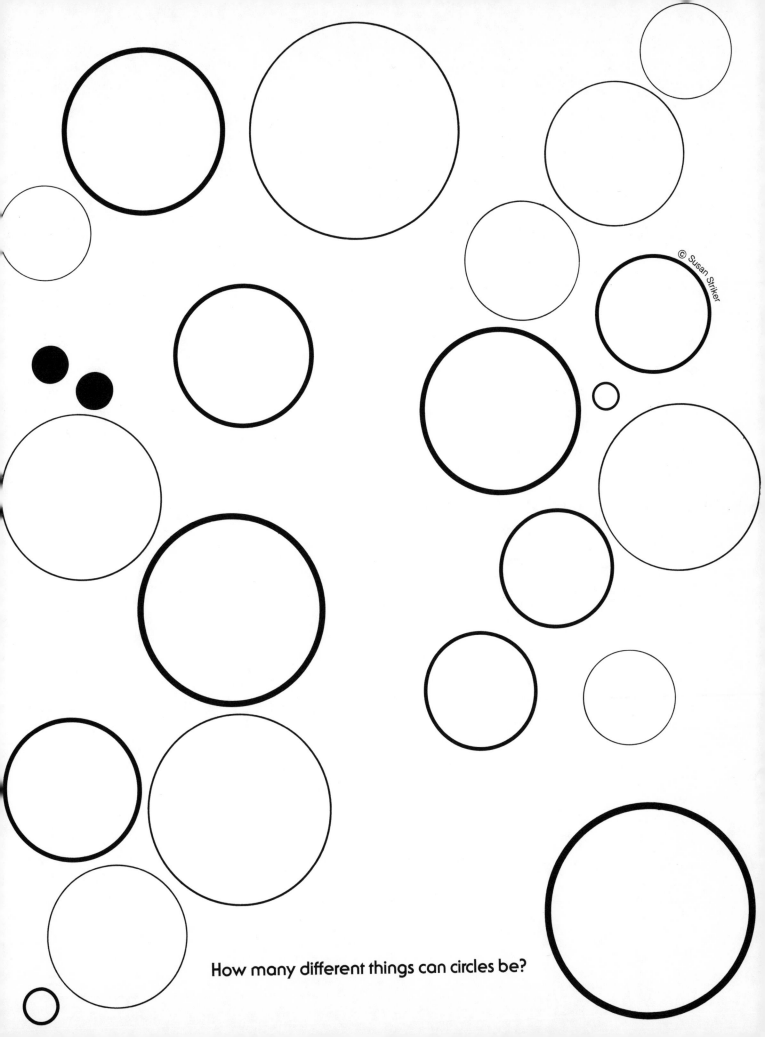

How many different things can circles be?

What important things would you like to talk about with your parents?

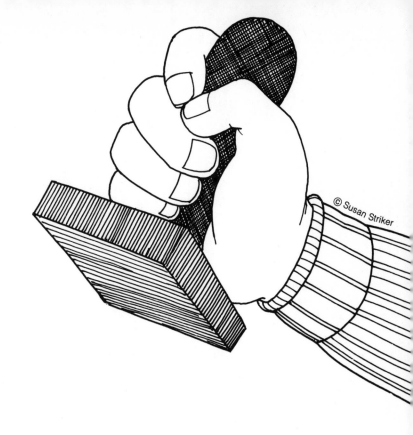

Design a secret seal, for only you to use,
that expresses something personal about yourself.

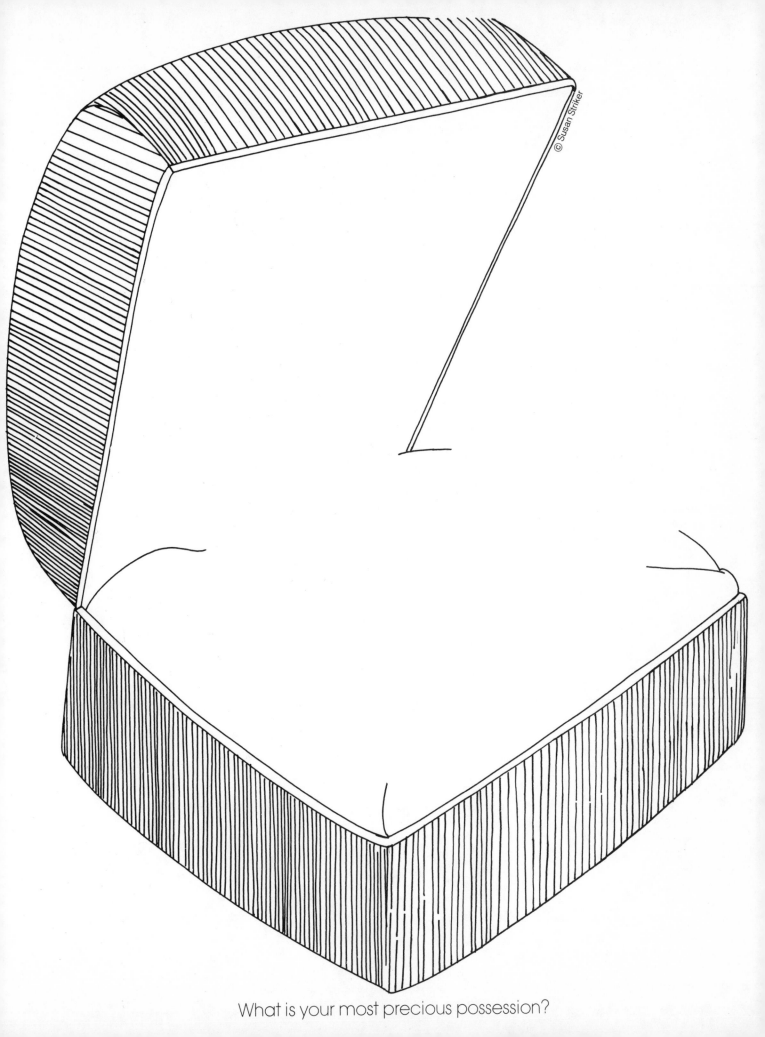

What is your most precious possession?

You are the manager of the biggest new singing group. What costumes and make-up will they wear for their performance?

© Susan Striker

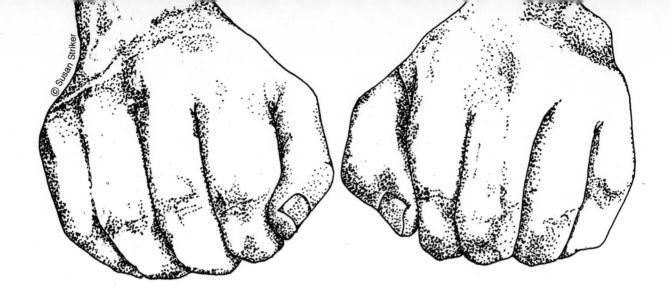

What surprise is hidden in the hands?

Make a wish on this wishing well.

© Susan Striker

Your ice sculpture has won first prize at the Winter Carnival.

Take a portrait of your family.

Put on a bubble show!

PETALUMA, CALIFORNIA ANNUAL UGLY DOG CONTEST

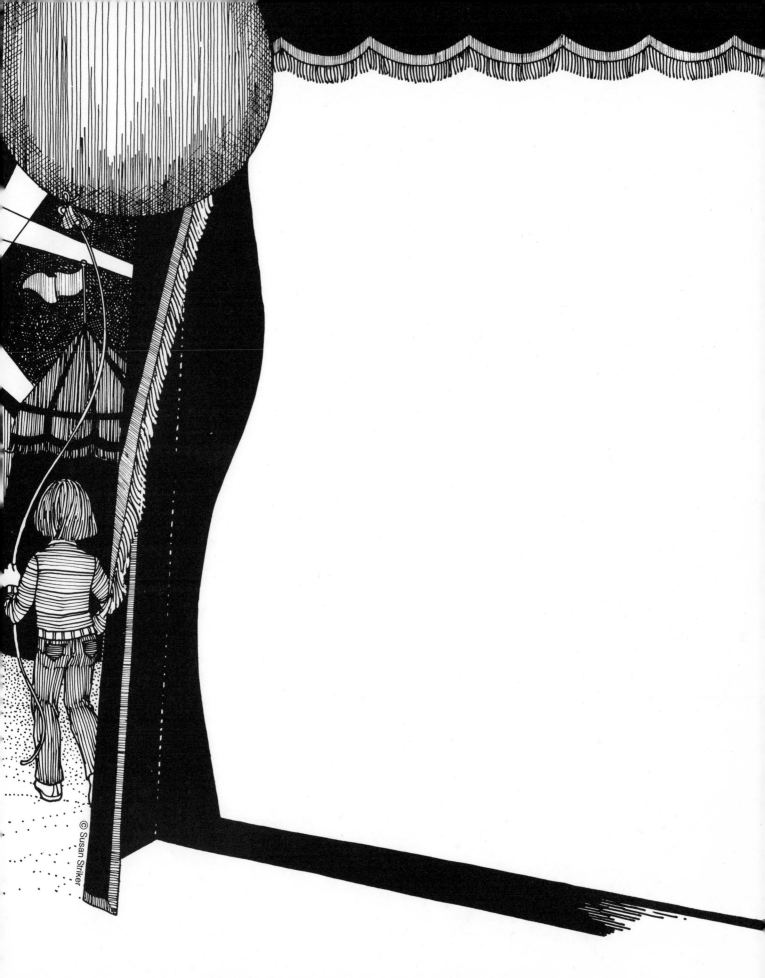

What do you look like in the fun-house mirror?

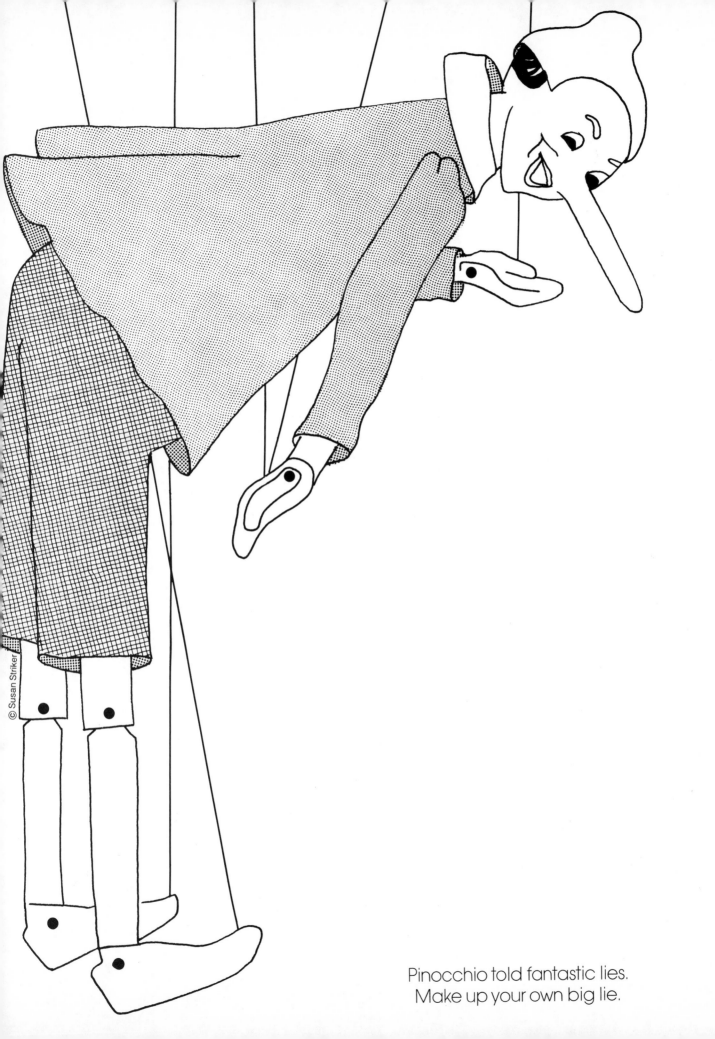

Pinocchio told fantastic lies.
Make up your own big lie.

What is Grandma knitting?

You have discovered an exciting
new animal.   What do you call it,
and what does it look like?

What kind of adventures do you remember from your past life as a pirate?

What is it that makes you angriest at your parents?

This cowhand is famous for doing dangerous stunts.

Why are these police officers writing out a ticket?

You have been hired to design a new subway token.

At show and tell you thrilled your class by bringing in the most exciting thing in the world.

PUPPET SHOW

If you owned an exotic pet shop,
what animals would you have in it?

© Susan Striker

What was the best game your mother or father
played with you when you were a baby?

© Susan Striker

What's going on up there?

© Susan Striker

**Mirror, mirror, on the wall,
who's the fairest of them all?**

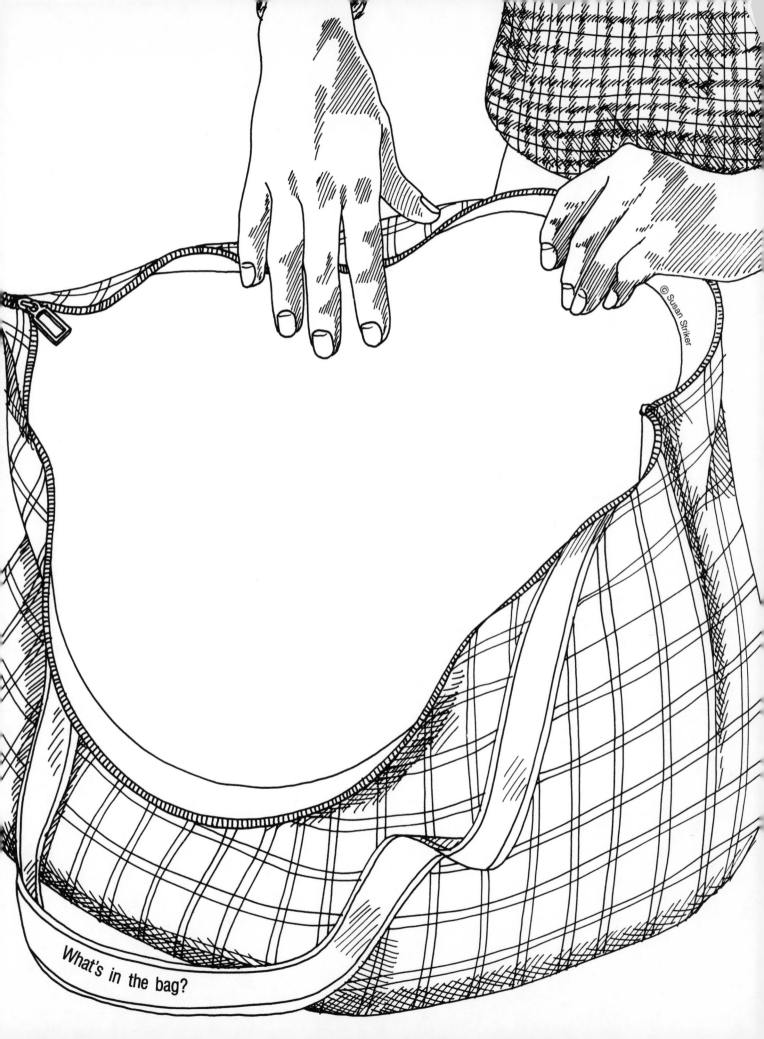

What's in the bag?

You have invented the
most popular new videogame.

© Susan Striker

**You are a reporter covering the
headline story of the year.**

Decorate this mug to give to someone you like.

© Susan Striker

**You have chartered a boat
to sail to Paradise.**

What is your favorite bedtime story?

If your rocket ship flew 100,000 miles straight up,
and then 100,000 miles east, where do you imagine you would be?

These people are admiring the statue
you built in the park.

Design your own train set.

What makes you laugh when you see old films of your family?

You have developed a new superspecies of plant.

Everyone in this art class is painting
something completely different.

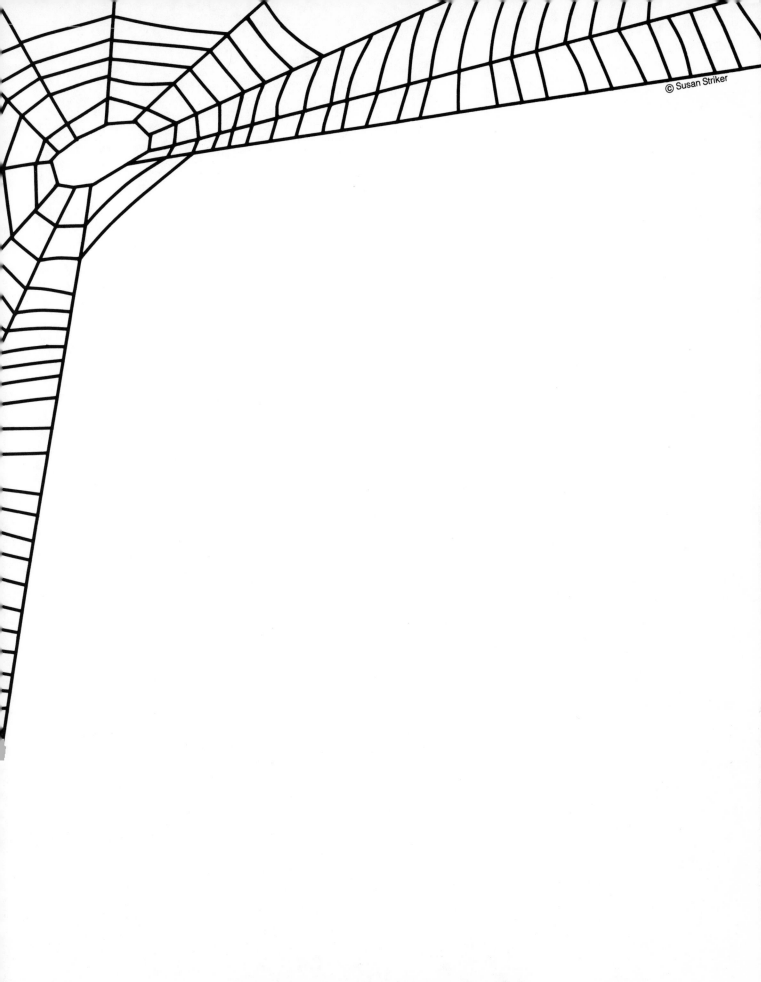

© Susan Striker

What did the spider catch in the web?

A collage is made with paste and paper scraps. Get out your collage materials, and have fun!